Excellent Advice *for* Living

ALSO BY KEVIN KELLY

Out of Control:
The New Biology of Machines, Social Systems
and the Economic World

New Rules for the New Economy:
10 Radical Strategies for a Connected World

What Technology Wants

Cool Tools:
A Catalog of Possibilities

The Silver Cord:
A Graphic Novel

The Inevitable:
Understanding the 12 Technological Forces
That Will Shape Our Future

Vanishing Asia

Excellent Advice
for Living

*Wisdom I Wish I'd
Known Earlier*

KEVIN KELLY

Viking

VIKING
An imprint of Penguin Random House LLC
penguinrandomhouse.com

Copyright © 2023 by Kevin Kelly

Some of the advice in this book previously appeared on
the author's blog, *The Technium* (kk.org/thetechnium).

ISBN 9780593654521 (hardcover)
ISBN 9780593654538 (ebook)

Printed in the United States of America
1st Printing

Designed by Amanda Dewey

Most of all, for my children:
Kaileen, Ting, and Tywen

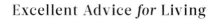

Excellent Advice *for* Living

O n my sixty-eighth birthday, I decided to give my young adult children some advice. I am not a frequent advice giver but soon I was able to write down 68 bits. To my surprise, I had more to say than I thought. So for the next several years I wrote down a batch of advice on my birthday, and shared it with my family and friends. They wanted more. I kept going until I had about 450 bits of advice I wished I'd known when I was younger.

I am primarily channeling the wisdom of the ages. I am offering advice I have heard from others, or timeless knowledge repeated from the past, or a modern aphorism that matched my own experience. I doubt any of it is truly original, although I have tried to put everything in my own words. I think of these bits as seeds because each one of them could easily be expanded into a long essay. Indeed, I have spent most of my time writing by compressing these substantial lessons into as compact and tweetable forms as possible. You are encouraged to expand these seeds as you read to fill your own situation.

If you find these proverbs align with your experience, share them with someone younger than yourself.

—Kevin Kelly, Pacifica, California, 2023

Learn how to learn
from those you disagree with,
or even offend you.
See if you can find
the truth in what they believe.

⟨⟶ ◦ ● ◦ ⟵⟩

Being enthusiastic
is worth 25 IQ points.

⟨⟶ ◦ ● ◦ ⟵⟩

Listening well is a superpower.
While listening to someone you love,
keep asking them,
"Is there more?"
until there is no more.

Always demand a deadline
because it weeds out
the extraneous and the ordinary.
A deadline prevents you from trying
to make it perfect,
so you have to make it different.
Different is better.

⟢⎯⎯⎯ ◆ ⎯⎯⎯⟣

Don't be afraid
to ask a question
that may sound stupid,
because 99% of the time
everyone else is thinking
of the same question
and is too embarrassed to ask it.

Prototype your life.
Try stuff instead of making grand plans.

———— ◦ ❦ ◦ ————

When you forgive others,
they may not notice,
but you will heal.
Forgiveness is not something
we do for others;
it is a gift to ourselves.

The fact that you "can't do" something
can be embarrassing.
But if you are "learning to do" something,
that is admirable.
There are only tiny baby steps
between can't and learning.

⸻ ◦ ⸻

Don't measure your life
with someone else's ruler.

When someone tells you
what ticks them off,
they are telling you
what makes them tick.

Collecting things benefits you
only if you display your collection
prominently
and share it in joy with others.
The opposite of this is hoarding.

Taking a break
is not a sign of weakness
but a sign of strength.

⸺ ·◈· ⸺

A major part of travel
is to leave stuff behind.
The more you leave behind
the further you will advance.

⸺ ·◈· ⸺

You don't have to attend
every argument you are invited to.

A worthy goal for a year
is to learn enough about a subject
so that you can't believe
how ignorant you were
a year earlier.

You can't reason
someone out of a notion
that they didn't reason themselves into.

Gratitude will unlock all other virtues
and is something you can get better at.

When you are anxious
because of your to-do list,
take comfort in your have-done list.

Treating a person to a meal never fails
and is so easy to do.
It's powerful with old friends
and a great way to make new friends.

Pain is inevitable. Suffering is optional.

If you are looking
for something in your house
and you finally find it,
when you're done with it,
don't put it back where you found it.
Put it back
where you first looked for it.

———— · ❀ · ————

Movement plus variety equals health.

Never use a credit card for credit.
The only kind of credit, or debt,
that is acceptable
is debt to acquire something
whose exchange value
is extremely likely to increase,
like a home.
The exchange value of most things
diminishes
or vanishes the moment
you purchase them.
Don't be in debt to losers.

⌐⟝◈⟞⌐

A great way to understand yourself
is to seriously reflect on everything
you find irritating in others.

The advantage
of a ridiculously ambitious goal
is that it sets the bar very high
so even if your effort falls short,
it may exceed an ordinary success.

⁌ ⁕ ⁍

When you give away 10% of your income,
you lose 10% of your purchasing power,
which is minor compared to the
110% increase in happiness you will gain.

The best way to learn anything
is to try to teach what you know.

⸺ ⸱ ❦ ⸱ ⸺

Whenever you have a choice between
being right or being kind,
be kind. No exceptions.
Don't confuse kindness with weakness.

⸺ ⸱ ❦ ⸱ ⸺

We lack rites of passage.
Create a memorable family ceremony
when your child reaches legal adulthood,
between eighteen and twenty-one.
This moment will become
a significant touchstone in their life.

The best way to get to yes in a negotiation
is to truly understand
what yes means for the other party.

Recipe for greatness:
Become just a teeny bit better
than you were last year.
Repeat every year.

Draw to discover what you see.
Write to discover what you think.

Whenever you can't decide
which path to take,
pick the one that produces change.

The quickest checkout line
will be the one with the fewest people,
no matter the size of their carts.

Choose not to be outraged today.

Habit is far more dependable
than inspiration.
Make progress by making habits.
Don't focus on getting into shape.
Focus on becoming the kind of person
who never misses a workout.

If you are the smartest person
in the room, you are in the wrong room.
Hang out with, and learn from,
people smarter than yourself.
Even better, find smart people
who will disagree with you.

You should demand
extraordinary evidence
in order to believe extraordinary claims.

Rule of 3 in conversation:
To get to the real reason, ask a person to go
deeper than what they just said.
Then again, and then once more.
The third time's answer
is the one closest to the truth.

Pros make as many mistakes as amateurs;
they've just learned how to
gracefully recover from their mistakes.

Don't be the best. Be the only.

Everyone is shy.
Other people are waiting for you
to introduce yourself to them;
they are waiting for you
to send them an email;
they are waiting for you
to ask them on a date.
Go ahead.

The more you are interested in others,
the more interesting they'll find you.
To be interesting, be interested.

Don't take it personally
when someone turns you down.
Assume they are like you:
busy, occupied, distracted.
Try again later. It's amazing
how often a second try works.

The purpose of a habit
is to remove that action
from self-negotiation.
You no longer expend energy
deciding whether to do it.
You just do it.
Good habits can range
from telling the truth to flossing.

Promptness is a sign of respect.

When you are young, spend
at least 6 months to 1 year
living as cheaply as you can,
owning as little as you possibly can,
eating beans and rice in a tiny room
or tent.
That way any time you have to risk
something in the future, you won't be afraid
of the "worst-case" scenario.

Trust me: There is no "them."

Tend to the small things.
More people are defeated by blisters
than by mountains.

You lead by letting others know
what you expect of them,
which may exceed what they
themselves expect.
Provide them a reputation
that they can step up to.

If you ask for someone's feedback,
you'll get a critic.
But if instead you ask for advice,
you'll get a partner.

The Golden Rule will never fail you.
It is the foundation of all other virtues.

To make something good, just do it.
To make something great, just redo it,
redo it, redo it.
The secret to making fine things
is in remaking them.

This is true:

It's hard to cheat an honest person.

⌐——— · ◈ · ———⌐

Expand your mind

by thinking with your feet on a walk

or with your hand in a notebook.

Think outside your brain.

⌐——— · ◈ · ———⌐

At first, buy the

absolute cheapest tools you can find.

Upgrade the ones you use a lot.

If you wind up using some tool for a job,

buy the very best you can afford.

Shorten your to-do list

by asking yourself,

"What is the worst that will happen

if this does not get done?"

Eliminate all but the disasters.

⌒⌒⌒⌒ · ❦ · ⌒⌒⌒⌒

To move through a place you may not be

permitted, act like you belong there.

Nothing elevates a person higher than
taking responsibility for their mistakes.
If you mess up, fess up.
It's astounding how powerful
this ownership is.

───── ◦ ⊕ ◦ ─────

Hatred is a curse
that does not affect the hated.
It only poisons the hater.
Release a grudge as if it were a poison.

───── ◦ ⊕ ◦ ─────

Don't take a job
because it pays the most money.

You can obsess about your customers
or you can obsess about
beating the competition.
Both work, but of the two,
obsessing about your customers
will take you further.

"No" is an acceptable
answer even without a reason.

Separate the processes of creating
from improving.
You can't write and edit,
or sculpt and polish,
or make and analyze at the same time.
If you do, the editor stops the creator.
While you invent, don't select.
While you sketch, don't inspect.
While you write the first draft, don't reflect.
At the start, the creator mind must be
unleashed from judgment.

<hr />

If you are not falling down occasionally,
you are just coasting.

Perhaps the most counterintuitive
truth of the universe
is that the more you give to others,
the more you'll get.
Understanding this
is the beginning of wisdom.

Keep showing up.
99% of success is just showing up.
In fact, most success is just persistence.

Friends are better than money.
Almost anything money can do,
friends can do better.
In so many ways, a friend with a boat
is better than owning a boat.

⌐——— ·◇· ———⌐

When an object is lost, 95% of the time
it is hiding within arm's reach
of where it was last seen.
Search in all possible locations
in that radius
and you'll find it.

A vacation + a disaster = an adventure.

Don't be in haste.
When you are in a hurry
you are more easily
conned or manipulated.

Forgiveness is accepting
the apology you will never get.

To cultivate a habit switch your
language from "I can or can't do"
to "I do or don't do."
You shift the weight
from a wavering choice
to an unwavering identity.

Be more generous than necessary.
No one on their deathbed has ever
regretted giving too much away.
There is no point to being
the richest person in the cemetery.

You need teachers, parents, customers, fans, and friends because they will see who you are becoming before you will.

❦

There is no limit on how much we can improve what we start with. There is no limit on better.

Be prepared: When you have 90%
of a large project completed,
finishing the final details
will take another 90%.
Houses and films are famous
for having two 90%s.

———•◦•———

Before you are old,
attend as many funerals as you can bear,
and listen. Nobody talks
about the departed's achievements.
The only thing people will remember
is what kind of person you were
while you were achieving.

Anything real begins with the fiction

of what could be.

Imagination is therefore

the most potent force in the universe.

And you can get better at it.

It's the one skill in life that benefits from

ignoring what everyone else knows.

———

When crises strike,

don't waste them.

No problems, no progress.

You really don't want to be famous.
Read the biography of any famous person.

On vacation go to the most remote place on
your itinerary first,
bypassing the cities,
and then return to the big city at the end.
You'll maximize the shock of otherness in
the remote, and then later
you'll welcome the familiar conveniences of a
busy city on the way back.

When you get invited
to do something in the future,
ask yourself: Would I do this tomorrow?
Not too many promises will pass
that immediacy filter.

Don't say anything about someone in email
you would not be comfortable
saying to them directly
because eventually it *will* reach them.

If you ask to be hired
mainly because you need a job,
you are just another problem for the boss;
if you can solve many of the problems the
boss has right now,
you are hired.
To be hired, think like your boss.

⸻ · ◦ · ⸻

It is not a compliment
if it comes with a request.

⸻ · ◦ · ⸻

Art is in
what you leave out.

Acquiring things
will rarely bring you deep satisfaction.
But acquiring experiences will.

⌐——·◦·——⌐

You are what you do.
Not what you say,
not what you believe,
not how you vote,
but what you spend your time on.

Rule of 7 in research:

You can find out anything

if you are willing to go seven levels.

If the first source you ask doesn't know,

ask them who you should ask next,

and so on down the line.

If you are willing to go to the seventh source,

you'll almost always get your answer.

———— · ◈ · ————

To earn bliss,

just for a moment,

send someone you don't know

a compliment for something they did.

When someone is
nasty, hateful, or mean toward you,
treat their behavior like
an affliction or illness they have.
That makes it easier to
have empathy toward them,
which can soften the conflict.

Eliminating clutter
makes room for your true treasures.

Don't ever respond to a solicitation or a
proposal on the phone.
The urgency is a disguise for a scam.

Experience is overrated. Most
breakthrough accomplishments were done by
people doing them for the first time.
Therefore when hiring,
hire for aptitude and attitude
and then train for skills.

How to apologize:
quickly, specifically, sincerely.
Don't ruin an apology with an excuse.

Don't bother asking a barber
if you need a haircut.
Pay attention to incentives.

That thing that made you weird as a kid
could make you great as an adult
—if you don't lose it.

Following your bliss

is a recipe for paralysis if you don't know

what you are passionate about.

A better path for most youth is

"master something."

Through mastery of one thing,

you'll command a viewpoint

to steadily find where your bliss is.

⟜————◈————⟜

To quiet a crowd or a drunk, just whisper.

When you lend something,
pretend you are gifting.
If it is returned,
you'll be surprised and happy.

⌐———·◦·———⌐

You are never too young
to wonder,
"Why am I still doing this?"
You need to have
an excellent answer.

A balcony or porch
needs to be at least 6 feet (2 meters) deep
or it won't be used.

Life gets better as you
replace transactions with relationships.

Investing small amounts of money

over a long time

works miracles,

but no one wants to get rich slow.

⸻ ❋ ⸻

The main thing

is to keep the main thing

the main thing.

⸻ ❋ ⸻

When in doubt, overtip.

To build strong children,
reinforce their sense
of belonging to a family
by articulating exactly what is
distinctive about your family.
They should be able to say with pride,
"Our family does X."

If you are not embarrassed
by your past self,
you have probably not grown up yet.

Outlaw the word "you"
during domestic arguments.

If you have any doubt at all
about being able to carry a load in one trip,
do yourself a huge favor
and make two trips.

⌐———·❖·———¬

Over the long term,
the future is decided by optimists.
To be an optimist you don't have to ignore
the multitude of problems we create;
you just have to imagine
how much our ability
to solve problems improves.

Don't let someone else's urgency
become your emergency.
In fact, don't be governed
by the urgent of any sort.
Focus on the important.
The urgent is a tyrant.
The important should be your king.
Down with the tyranny of the urgent!

Learn how to take a 20-minute power nap
without embarrassment.

Paradoxically, the
worst evils in the world
are committed by those
who truly believe they are combating evil.
Be extremely vigilant with *yourself*
when facing evil.

Don't reserve you kindest praise
for a person until their eulogy.
Tell them while they are alive,
when it makes a difference to them,
Write it in a letter they can keep.

Fear is fueled by a lack of imagination.
The antidote to fear is not bravery;
it looks more like imagination.

Train employees well enough
that they could get another job,
but treat them well enough
that they never want to.

If it fails where you thought it would fail,
that is not a failure.

Superheroes and saints
never make art.
Only imperfect beings can make art
because art begins in what is broken.

If someone is trying to convince you
it's not a pyramid scheme,
it's a pyramid scheme.

Don't create things to make money;
make money so you can create things.
The reward for good work is more work.

Leave a gate behind you
the way you first found it.

In 100 years
a lot of what we take to be true now
will be proved to be wrong, maybe even
embarrassingly wrong.
A good question to ask yourself today is,
"What might I be wrong about?"
This is the only worry worth having.

———•❦•———

Learn how to tie a bowline knot.
Practice in the dark. With one hand.
For the rest of your life you'll use this knot
more times than you would ever believe.

The greatest rewards
come from working on something that
nobody has words for.
If you possibly can,
work where there are no names
for what you do.

On the way to a grand goal,
celebrate the smallest victories
as if each one were the final goal.
That way, no matter where it ends
you are victorious.

In all things—except love—
start with the exit strategy.
Prepare for the ending.
Almost anything is easier to get into
than out of.

Don't aim to have others like you;
aim to have them respect you.

The foundation of maturity:
Just because it's not your fault
doesn't mean it's not your responsibility.

A multitude of bad ideas
is necessary for one good idea.

———

The hard part in predicting the future
is to forget everything
you expect it to be.

———

Compliment people behind their back.
It'll come back to you.

Most overnight successes
—in fact, any significant successes—
take at least 5 years.
Budget your life accordingly.

The job of a grandparent
is to grandparent, not to parent.
Parent's house, parent rules.
Grandparent's house, grandparent rules.

You don't need more time because
you already have all the time
that you will ever get;
you need more focus.

The foolish person winds up
doing at the end what
the smart person does
at the beginning.

For marital bliss,
take turns allowing each partner
to be always right.

If the cost of something
is not advertised,
it is a sign that it's
more than you can afford.

Everyone's time is finite and shrinking.
The highest leverage
you can get with your money
is to buy someone else's time.
Hire and outsource when you can.

Your best response to an insult is
"You're probably right."
Often they are.

Assume anyone asking for your account
information for any reason
is guilty of scamming you,
unless proven innocent.
The way to prove innocence is to call
them back, or log in to your account using
numbers or a website that you provide,
not them. Don't release any identifying
information while they are contacting you
via phone, message, or email.
You must control the channel.

⌐⌐⌐⌐ · ⦿ · ⌐⌐⌐⌐

Fear makes people do stupid things,
so don't trust anything made in fear.

Be strict with yourself, forgiving of others.
The reverse is hell for everyone.

⎯⎯ ⎯ ✦ ⎯ ⎯⎯

If you can avoid seeking the approval of others,
your power is limitless.

⎯⎯ ⎯ ✦ ⎯ ⎯⎯

Your passions should fit you exactly,
but your purpose in life should exceed you.
Work for something
much larger than yourself.

When a child asks an endless string of "Why?" questions, the smartest reply is "I don't know, what do you think?"

⸻

Recipe for success: underpromise and overdeliver.

Show me your calendar
and I will tell you your priorities.
Tell me who your friends are
and I'll tell you where you're going.

⌒‿‿‿ ⁕ ❀ ⁕ ‿‿‿⌒

When brainstorming,
improvising,
jamming with others,
you'll go much further and deeper
if you build upon each contribution
with a playful "yes—and" example
instead of a deflating "no—but" reply.

Work to become, not to acquire.

Contemplating the weaknesses of others
is easy;
contemplating the weaknesses in yourself
is hard,
but it pays a much higher reward.

When you are young,
have friends who are older;
when you are old,
have friends who are younger.

You will complete your mission in life when

you figure out

what your mission in life is.

Your purpose is to discover your purpose.

This is not a paradox.

This is the way.

⌒⌒⌒⌒⌒ ⊙ ⌒⌒⌒⌒⌒

With sharp things,

always cut away from yourself.

Calm is contagious. Be calm to help others.

When someone tells you something is
wrong, they're usually right.
When they tell you how to fix it,
they're usually wrong.

You are only as young
as the last time you changed your mind.

When hitchhiking,
look like the person you want
to pick you up.

Worth repeating: Measure twice, cut once.

⌐———— ⁃ ✦ ⁃ ————¬

Money is overrated.
Truly new things rarely need an abundance
of money. If that was so, billionaires
would have a monopoly on inventing new
things, and they don't. Instead, almost all
breakthroughs are made by those who
lack money. If breakthroughs could be
bought, then the rich would buy them.
Instead, passion, persistence, belief, and
ingenuity are required to invent new things,
qualities the poor and young often have in
abundance. Stay hungry.

If you can't tell what you desperately need,
it's probably sleep.

Ignore what others may be thinking of you
because they aren't thinking of you.

⸻ ◦ ⸻

Writing down one thing
you are grateful for each day
is the cheapest possible therapy ever.

If you meet a jerk, ignore them.
If you meet jerks everywhere every day,
look deeper into yourself.

It is much easier
to change how you think
by changing your behavior
than it is to change your behavior
by changing how you think.
Act out the change you seek.

If you think you saw a mouse, you did.
And if there is one, there are more.

Don't worry how or where you begin.
As long as you keep moving, your
success will arrive far from where you start.

Avoid hitting the snooze button.
That's just training you to oversleep.

You'll learn a lot more
if you ask people
"how are you sleeping?"
instead of "how are you doing?"

Generally, say less than necessary.

Each time you connect to people,
bring them a blessing;
then they'll be happy to see you
when you bring them a problem.

Even in the tropics it gets colder at night
than you think. Pack warmly.

⸻ ⋅ ❦ ⋅ ⸻

The work on any worthy project is
endless, infinite.
You cannot limit the work
so you must limit your hours.
Your time, not the work,
is the only thing you can manage.

You can reduce the annoyance
of someone's stupid belief
by increasing your understanding
of why they believe it.

＊

This is the best time ever
to make something.
None of the greatest, coolest creations 20
years from now have been invented yet.
You are not late.

To transcend the influence of your heroes,
copy them shamelessly like a student
until you get them out of your system.
That is the way of all masters.

Things do not need to be perfect
to be wonderful.
Especially weddings.

When you are stuck, sleep on it.
Give your subconscious an assignment
while you sleep.
You'll have an answer in the morning.

All the greatest prizes in life
in wealth, relationships, or knowledge
come from the magic
of compounding interest,
by amplifying small steady gains.
All you need for abundance is
to keep adding 1% more than you subtract
on a regular basis.

You can eat any dessert you want
if you take only three bites.

Don't treat people as bad as they are.

Treat them as good as you are.

Children totally accept
—and crave—family rules.
"In our family we have a rule for X"
is the only excuse a parent needs
for setting a family policy.
In fact, "I have a rule for X"
is the only excuse you need
for your own personal policies.

When you confront a stuck bolt or screw:
righty tighty, lefty loosey.

Bad things can happen fast,
but almost all good things happen slowly.

We are not a body
that carries a soul.
We are a soul that is assigned a body,
not of our choosing, but in our care.

If your goal does not have a schedule,

it is a dream.

Be a good ancestor.
Do something a future generation
will thank you for.
A simple thing is to plant a tree.

———— ⋅✦⋅ ————

People can't remember
more than three points from a speech.

The greatest breakthroughs are missed
because they look like really hard work.

To be remarkable, read books.

Finite games are played
to win or lose.
Infinite games are played
to keep the game going.
Seek out infinite games
because they yield unlimited rewards.

To succeed, get other people to pay you;
to become wealthy, help other people
to succeed.

───── · ❦ · ─────

Your behavior, not your opinions,
will change the world.

───── · ❦ · ─────

A problem that can easily be solved with money
is not really a problem
because
its solution is obvious.
Focus on problems with non-obvious solutions.

Every person you meet
knows an amazing lot about something
you know virtually nothing about.
It won't be obvious,
and your job is to discover what it is.

Cultivate an allergy to average.

To combat an adversary,
become their friend.

If you are buying stock, the person selling
it thinks it is worth less than you do.
If you are selling, they think it is
worth more than you do.
Each time you are ready to
buy or sell stock,
ask yourself,
"What do I know that they don't?"

You don't marry a person,
you marry a family.

Be nice to your children because they are
going to choose your nursing home.

· ❦ ·

About 99% of the time,
the right time is right now.

· ❦ ·

All guns are loaded.

Cultivate 12 people who love you,
because they are worth more
than 12 million people who like you.

Always be quick to give credit,
and to take blame.

Be frugal in all things,
except in your passions.
Select a few interests
that you gleefully splurge on.
In fact, be all-around thrifty
so that you can splurge on your passions.

To manage yourself use your head;
to manage others use your heart.

⌒⌒⌒⌒ · ❦ · ⌒⌒⌒⌒

Dance with your hips.

⌒⌒⌒⌒ · ❦ · ⌒⌒⌒⌒

Don't let your email inbox
become your to-do list run by others.

The best way to untangle a knotty tangle is not to "untie" the knots but to keep pulling the loops apart wider and wider. Just make the mess as big, loose, and open as possible. As you open up the knots, they will unravel themselves. Works on cords, strings, hoses, yarns, or electronic cables.

Take one simple thing
—almost anything—
but take it extremely seriously,
as if it is the only thing in the world
—or maybe the entire world is in it—
and by taking it seriously
you'll light up the sky.

When making something,
always get a few extras—extra material,
extra parts, extra space, extra finishes.
The extras serve as backups for mistakes,
reduce stress,
and fill your inventory for the future.
They are the cheapest insurance.

No one is as impressed with your
possessions as you are.

Don't ever work for someone
you don't want to become.

No secrets. You are much better off
delivering unwelcome news
to someone yourself directly.
A secret is rarely unknown, which means
inevitably someone else will share it.
Meanwhile, the secret
corrodes all who hold it.
Resist accepting secrets.

The expanding universe is
overflowing with abundance.
It is so full that improvement can often be
gained only by subtracting.
Keep removing, until you can't.
End with wanting more, not less.

Figure out what time of day you are most productive and protect that time period.

Experiences are fun,
and having influence is rewarding,
but only mattering makes us happy.
Do stuff that matters.

Greatness is incompatible with
optimizing in the short term.
To achieve greatness
requires a long view.
Raise your time horizon to raise your goal.

Most wonderful things
quickly become unwonderful
if they are repeated too often.
Once-in-a-life is often the optimal interval.

When you open paint,
even a tiny bit, it will always find its way to
your clothes no matter how careful you are.
Dress accordingly.

———— · ◈ · ————

You have to first follow the rules
with diligence in order to
break them productively.

———— · ◈ · ————

If you stop to listen to a musician
or street performer for more than a minute,
you owe them a dollar.

Learning probability and statistics
is far more useful
than learning algebra and calculus.

If winning
becomes too important in a game,
change the rules to make it more fun.
Changing rules can become the new game.

The greatest teacher is called "doing."

Anything you say before the word "but" does not count.

⌐———— · ◈ · ————⌐

Courtesy costs nothing.
When you borrow something, return it
cleaned. Lower the toilet seat after use.
Let the car in front of you merge. Return
shopping carts to their designated areas.
Let the people in the elevator
exit before you enter.
These courtesies are free.

Whenever there is an argument between
two sides,
find the third side.

⌐——·⊛·——⌐

The consistency of your endeavors
(exercise, companionship, work)
is more important than the quantity.
Nothing beats small things done every day,
which is way more important
than what you do occasionally.

When you lead,
your real job is to create more leaders,
not more followers.

It is the duty of a teacher
to get everything out of a student,
and the duty of a student
to get everything out of a teacher.

Efficiency is highly overrated;
goofing off is highly underrated.
Regularly scheduled sabbaths, sabbaticals,
vacations, breaks, aimless walks,
and time off are essential for top
performance of any kind.
The best work ethic
requires a good rest ethic.

Speak confidently as if you are right,

but listen carefully as if you are wrong.

Productivity is often a distraction.
Don't aim for better ways to get through
your tasks as quickly as possible.
Instead aim for better tasks
that you never want to stop doing.

———— · ● · ————

Your enjoyment of travel is inversely
proportional to the size of your luggage.
This is 100% true of backpacking.
It is liberating to realize
how little you really need.

Ask funders for money,
and they'll give you advice;
but ask for advice,
and they'll give you money.

⸺ ⁂ ⸺

The biggest lie we tell ourselves is
"I don't need to write this down
because I will remember it."

Criticize in private, praise in public.

Don't keep making the same **mistakes**;
try to make new mistakes.

Your growth as a mature being
is measured by the number of
uncomfortable conversations
you are willing to have.

Handy measure: The distance between the
fingertips of your outstretched arms
at shoulder level is roughly your height.

Don't buy anything late at night.
There is nothing you need to buy that
cannot wait till tomorrow morning.

When you have good news
and bad news, give the bad news first,
because we remember how things
end more than how they begin.
So elevate the ending with good news.

⎯⎯⎯ ◦ ⚬ ◦ ⎯⎯⎯

Immediately pay what you owe
to vendors, workers, contractors.
If you do, they will go out of their way
to work with you first next time.

⎯⎯⎯ ◦ ⚬ ◦ ⎯⎯⎯

The four most powerful words in any
negotiation should be uttered by you:
"Can you do better?"

Three things you need:
the ability to not give up something
till it works,
the ability to give up something
that does not work,
and the trust in other people to help you
distinguish between the two.

You can find no better medicine
for your family
than regular meals together
without screens.

There is no such thing as being "on time."
Either you are late or you are early.
Your choice.

Making art is not selfish;
it's for the rest of us.
If you don't do your thing,
you are cheating us.

In a genuine survival situation,
you can go 3 weeks without food,
and 3 days without water,
but only 3 hours without warmth or shade.
So don't worry about food.
Focus on temperature and water.

When you are in the wrong,
be quick to chastise yourself more severely
than the aggrieved might.
Paradoxically, this can soften their ire.

Learn how to be alone without being lonely.
Solitude is essential for creativity.

⁖

When you feel like quitting,
just do five more:
5 more minutes, 5 more pages,
5 more steps. Then repeat. Sometimes
you can break through and keep going,
but even if you can't, you ended five ahead.
Tell yourself that you will quit tomorrow,
but not today.

Never ask someone if they are pregnant.

Let them tell you.

What you do on your bad days
matters more
than what you do on your good days.

⎯⎯⎯ · ❈ · ⎯⎯⎯

Ask anyone you admire:
Their lucky breaks happened on a detour
from their main goal.
So embrace detours.
Life is not a straight line for anyone.

To be rich
you don't need to make more money;
you chiefly need to better manage
the money already flowing
through your hands.

———— ⁂ ————

When speaking to an audience,
pause frequently.
Pause before you say
something in a new way,
pause after you have said something
you believe is important,
and pause as a relief
to let listeners absorb details.

The best way to get a correct answer
on the internet is
to post an obviously wrong answer
and wait for someone to correct you.

———— · ◆ · ————

You'll get 10 times better results
by elevating good behavior
rather than punishing bad behavior,
especially in children and animals.

Spend as much time crafting the subject
line of an email as the message itself,
because the subject line is often
the only thing people read.

───── ⁘ ─────

When you're checking references for a job
applicant, their employer may be prohibited
from saying anything negative,
so leave or send a message that says,
"Get back to me if you highly recommend
this applicant as super great."
If they don't reply, take that as a negative.

Don't wait for the storm to pass;
dance in the rain.

Make stuff that is good for people to have.

Keep all your things visible
in a hotel room, not in drawers
and all gathered into one spot. That way
you'll never leave anything behind.
If you need to have something like a
charger off to the side,
place a couple of other large items next to
it, because you are less likely
to leave three items behind than just one.

Denying or deflecting a compliment
is rude. Accept it with thanks,
even if you believe it is not deserved.

Always read the plaque
next to the monument.

When you have some success, the feeling of
being an imposter can be real.
Who am I fooling?
But when you create things that only you
with your unique talents
and experience can do,
then you are absolutely not an imposter.
You are the ordained.
It is your destiny to work
on things that only you can do.

To keep young kids behaving well
on a car road trip, have a bag
of their favorite unwrapped candy
and throw a piece out the window
each time they misbehave.

⸻ • ❈ • ⸻

When you don't know how much
to pay someone for a particular task,
ask them, "What would be fair?"
and their answer usually is.

The general strategy for real estate
is to buy the worst property
on the best street.

You cannot get smart people to work
extremely hard just for money.

Half the skill of being educated
is learning what you can ignore.

If you're doing something
that you are hiding from others,
it's probably not good for you.

⌐⸏⸏⸏ ˙◦˙ ⸏⸏⸏⌐

When you need to cut something
extremely exact,
don't try to do it with one cut.
Instead, cut it a bit bigger and then keep
trimming it bit by bit until perfect.
Professional makers call this "creeping up"
to the precise measurement.

Make others feel they are important; it will make their day and it will make your day.

───── ·◦· ─────

Constantly search for
overlapping areas of agreement
and dwell there.
Disagreements will appear to be edge cases.

───── ·◦· ─────

90% of everything is crap.
If you think you don't like opera, romance
novels, TikTok, country music, vegan food,
NFTs, keep trying to see
if you can find the 10% that is not crap.

You will be judged on how well you treat those who can do nothing for you.

We tend to overestimate
what we can do in a day,
and underestimate
what we can achieve in a decade.
Miraculous things can be accomplished
if you give it 10 years.
A long game will compound small gains
that will be able to overcome
even big mistakes.

Let someone know
you remembered their name
and they won't ever forget yours.
To help remember their name,
repeat it on first hearing.

⟡

Your best job
will be one that you were unqualified for,
because it stretches you.
In fact, only apply to jobs
you are unqualified for.

You can be whatever you want to be,
so be the person who ends meetings early.

⸺ ⚬ ⸺

Buy used books.
They have the same words as the new ones.
Also, libraries.

A wise man said: Before you speak, let
your words pass through three gates.
At the first gate, ask yourself, "Is it true?"
At the second gate ask, "Is it necessary?"
At the third gate ask, "Is it kind?"

The only productive way to answer
"What should I do now?"
is to first tackle the question of
"Who should I become?"

When you board an airplane, arrive at your
room in a hotel, or start a new job, locate
the emergency exits.
It only takes a minute.

The best investing advice:
Average returns, maintained
for above-average periods of time,
will yield extraordinary results.
Buy and hold.

Take the stairs.

What you actually pay for something
can be twice the listed price
because the energy, time, and money needed
to set it up, learn, maintain, repair it,
and then dispose of it when done
all have their own cost.
Not all prices appear on labels.

If a young student is struggling,
first thing: Check their eyesight.

It's thrilling to be extremely polite
to rude strangers.

Most articles and stories
are improved significantly if you delete the
first page of the manuscript.
Start with the action.

Getting cheated occasionally
is the small price
for trusting the best of everyone,
because when you trust the best in others,
they generally treat you best.

It's possible that a not-so-smart person
who can communicate well
can do much better than a super-smart
person who can't communicate well.
That is good news
because it is much easier
to improve your communication skills
than your intelligence.

Take note if you find yourself wondering
"Where is my good knife?"
or "Where is my good pen?"
That means you have bad ones.
Get rid of those.

For the best results with your children,
spend only half the money
you think you should
but double the time with them.

Avoid wearing a hat
that has more character than you do.

Looking ahead, focus on direction
rather than destinations.
Maintain the right direction
and you'll arrive at where you want to go.

Art is whatever you can get away with.

Purchase the most recent tourist guidebook
to your hometown or region.
You'll learn a lot
by playing the tourist once a year.

To become a hero, thank a teacher
who made a difference in your life.

⌦ ⁃ ◆ ⁃ ⌫

When buying a garden hose, an extension
cord, or a ladder, get one substantially
longer than you think you need.
It'll be the right size.

When you are stuck,
explain your problem to others.
Often simply laying out a problem
will present a solution.
Make "explaining the problem"
part of your troubleshooting process.

⌐———— · ❀ · ————⌐

Don't wait in line to eat something famous.
It is rarely worth the wait.

⌐———— · ❀ · ————⌐

When introduced to someone,
make eye contact and count to four
or say to yourself, "I see you."
You'll both remember each other.

Your group can achieve great things
way beyond your means
simply by showing people
that they are appreciated.

———— ·◇· ————

Be a pro. Back up your backup.
Have at least one physical backup
and one backup in the cloud.
Have more than one of each.
How much would you pay to retrieve all
your data, photos, notes if you lost them?
Backups are cheap compared to regrets.

Prescription for popular success:

do something strange.

Make a habit of your weird.

~~~~~ ◈ ~~~~~

Your time and space are limited.

Remove, give away, throw out anything that

no longer gives you joy

in order to make room for those that do.

To signal an emergency,

use the rule of 3:

3 shouts, 3 horn blasts, or 3 whistles.

⎯⎯ ⚬ ⎯⎯

Don't compare your inside

to someone else's outside.

Explore or optimize?

Do you optimize what you know will sell
or explore with something new?
Do you order a restaurant dish
you are sure is great (optimize)
or do you try something new?
Do you keep dating new folks (explore)
or try to commit to someone you met?
The ideal balance for exploring new things
vs. optimizing those already found
is ⅓.
Spend ⅓ of your time on exploring and
⅔ on optimizing and deepening.
As you mature it is harder to devote time
to exploring because it seems unproductive,
but aim for ⅓.

Occasionally your first idea is best,
but usually it's the fifth idea.
You need to get all the obvious ideas
out of the way.
Try to surprise yourself.

Don't bother fighting the old,
just build the new.

Actual great opportunities will not have
"Great Opportunities" in the subject line.

When someone tells you
about the peak year of human history,
the period of time when things were good
before things went downhill,
it will always be the year
when they were 10 years old—
which is the peak of any human's existence.
Factor that into what they say.

⌐———— · ◈ · ————⌐

To rapidly reveal the true character
of a person you just met,
observe them stuck on
an abysmally slow internet connection.

In preparing for a long hike,
old shoes of any type are superior to
brand-new shoes of any type.
Don't use a long hike to break in shoes.

When negotiating,
don't aim for a bigger piece of the pie;
aim to create a bigger pie.

You are as big
as the things that make you angry.

You see only 2% of another person,
and they see only 2% of you.
Attune yourself to the hidden 98%.

Our descendants will achieve things
that will amaze us,
yet a portion of what they will create
could have been made with today's
materials and tools
if we had had the imagination.
Think bigger.

Do more of what looks like work to others
but is play for you.

Gemini

If you want something to get done,
ask a busy person to do it.

Gemini

Remember that repair tasks
take 3 times longer
than expected,
even when you expect them
to take 3 times longer.

Copying others
is a good way to start.
Copying yourself
is a disappointing way to end.

If you repeated what you did today
365 more times,
will you be where you want to be next year?

The best time to negotiate your salary
for a new job is the moment *after*
they say they want you,
and not before.
Then it becomes a game of chicken
for each side to name an amount first,
but it is to your advantage
to get them to give a number before you do.

Pay attention to
what you pay attention to.

For maximum results,
focus on your biggest opportunities,
not your biggest problems.

Every breakthrough
is at first laughable and ridiculous.
In fact, if it did not start out
laughable and ridiculous,
it is not a breakthrough.

Reading to your children regularly
is the best school they will ever get.

If you don't smoke before the age of 25
you are unlikely to ever start;
if you do smoke before 25
you are unlikely to ever quit.

It doesn't matter how many people
don't appreciate you or your work.
The only thing that counts is how many do.

It is far safer after a car accident
to remain in the car
rather than standing near it on the road,
where the accident increases
the chances of another accident.

When you are looking for a job, remember
that somewhere an employer is desperately
hunting for someone like you,
especially if you are unconventional.
Your real job is to make that match happen,
and it is worth whatever time it takes.

———— · ◉ · ————

Rather than steering your life
to avoid the unexpected,
aim directly for it.

Don't grocery shop while hungry.

If your opinions on one subject
can be predicted
from your opinions on another,
you may be in the grip of an ideology.
When you truly think for yourself,
your conclusions will not be predictable.

⌒─── • ❦ • ───⌒

You can really change someone's life for the better
simply by offering words of encouragement.

⌒─── • ❦ • ───⌒

When you are presented with a task that
could be completed in 2 minutes or less,
do it immediately.

The stronger your beliefs,
the stronger your reasons
to question them regularly.
Don't simply believe everything
you think you believe.

⸻

When a customer of yours complains,
always apologize first and ask,
"What can we do to resolve this?"
even if it is not your fault.
Acting as if the customer is right
is a small tax to pay to grow a business.

If you loan someone $20
and you never see them again
because they are avoiding paying you back,
that makes it worth $20.

A superpower worth cultivating
is learning from people you don't like.
It is called "humility."
This is the courage
to let dumb, stupid, hateful, crazy, mean
people teach you something,
because despite their character flaws,
they each know something you don't.

Don't purchase extra insurance
if you are renting a car with a credit card.

⌐━━━ ⋅✦⋅ ━━━⌐

For every good thing you love,
ask yourself what your proper dose is.

Hikers' rule:

Don't step on what you can step over;

don't step over what you can walk around.

———————

The trick to making wise decisions

is to evaluate your choices as if

you were looking back 25 years from today.

What would your future self think?

———————

To be interesting,

just tell your own story

with uncommon honesty.

When speaking to an audience,
it's better to fix your gaze on a few people
than to "spray" your gaze across the room.
Your eyes telegraph to others whether
you really believe what you are saying.

<hr/>

The main reason
to produce something every day
is that you must throw away
a lot of good work to reach the great stuff.
To let it all go easily,
you need to be convinced that
there is "more where that came from."
You get that in steady production.

The real test of your character

is not how you deal with adversity—

although that will teach you much.

The real test is how you deal with power.

The only cure for power is humility

and the admission that

your power comes from luck.

The small person believes they are superior;

the superior person knows they are lucky.

You will thrive more

—and so will others—

when you promote what you love

rather than bash what you hate.

Life is short; focus on the good stuff.

When sharing, one person divides,
the other chooses.

I t is easy to get trapped
by your own success.
Say no to tasks you probably won't fail at
and say yes to what you could fail at.

Unhappiness comes from
wanting what others have.
Happiness comes from
wanting what you already have.

When working with electricity,
volts hurt, but amps kill.

To get your message across,
follow this formula used by
ad writers everywhere:
simplify, simplify, simplify, then exaggerate.

Pay attention
to who you are around
when you feel your best.
Be with them more often.

Assume no one remembers names.
As a courtesy,
reintroduce yourself by name
even to those you have previously met:
"Hi, I'm Kevin."

What you do instead of work
might become your real work.

The very best thing
you can do for your kids
is to love your spouse.

Your golden ticket
is being able to see things
from other people's point of view.
This shift enables heartfelt empathy.
It also allows you to persuade others,
and it is the key to great design.
Mastering the view through the eyes of others
will unlock so many doors.

If you think that something
"goes without saying,"
it is usually best for everyone
if you just go ahead and say it.

To meditate, sit

and pay attention to your breathing.

Your mind will wander to thoughts.

Then you bring your attention back

to your breathing,

where it can't think.

Wander. Retreat.

Keep returning to breath,

no thoughts.

That is all.

Five years from now

you will wish you had started today.

If we all threw our troubles
into a big pile
and we saw everyone else's problems,
we would immediately grab ours back.

Your heart needs to be
as educated as your mind.

You can't change your past,
but you can change your story about it.
What is important is not
what happened to you but
what you *did* about what happened to you.

⸻ ⚬ ⸻

To have a great trip, head toward an
interest rather than to a place.
Travel to passions rather than destinations.

⸻ ⚬ ⸻

Let your children
choose their punishments.
They'll be tougher than you will.

In the garden,
dig a $100 hole for a $10 plant.

⸺ ◆ ⸺

Fully embrace
"What is the *worst* that can happen?"
at each juncture in life.
Rehearsing your response to the "worst" can
reveal it as an adventure
and rob it of its power to stall you.

Make one to throw away.
The only way to write a great book
is to first write an awful book.
Ditto for a movie, song, piece of furniture,
or anything.

For lofty goals, measure your progress from
where you started
rather than where you need to finish.

You increase your chance
of successfully removing a clothing stain
if you keep it wet while you work on it.
It's much harder once it dries out.

Anger is not the proper response to anger.
When you see someone angry
you are seeing their pain.
Compassion
is the proper response to anger.

When you find something you really enjoy,
do it slowly.

Ignore dogs that bark.
Look for the charging dog not barking.
That is the one who bites.

⌒〜〜 · ◈ · 〜〜⌒

Assuming you are average,
half of the world
will be less proficient than you.
Through no fault of their own,
many of these people can't handle forms,
complex instructions, or tricky situations.
Be kind to them because the world is not.

Your flaws and your strengths
are two poles of the same traits.
For instance, there is only
a tiny difference between
stubbornness and perseverance
or between courage and foolishness.
The sole difference is in the goal.
It's stupid stubbornness
and reckless foolishness
if the goal does not matter, and
relentless perseverance and
courage if it does.
To earn dignity with your flaws,
own up to them, and
make sure you push on things that matter.

The end is almost always
the beginning of something better.

⌒————·⚙·————⌒

It is impossible for you to become poor
by giving.
It is impossible for you to become wealthy
without giving.

Try hard
to solicit constructive criticism early.
You want to hear what's not working
as soon as possible.
When it is finished
you can't improve it.

⸻

To get better at speaking,
watch a recording of yourself speaking.
It is shocking and painful,
but an effective way to improve.

Don't attribute to malice
what can be explained by incompetence.

⁖

Worry is ineffective.
It is certain that 99% of the stuff
you are anxious about won't happen.

⁖

You can ignore any website
with the word "truth" in its URL.

Be extremely stingy in making promises
because you must be generous
in keeping them.

⊙

Don't mistake a clear view of the future
for a short distance.

⊙

A proper apology
consists of conveying the 3 Rs:
regret (genuine empathy with the other),
responsibility (not blaming someone else),
and remedy (your willingness to fix it).

The best way to advise young people
is to find out what they really want to do
and then advise them to do it.

It is usually much easier
to make big audacious changes
than small incremental ones.

The big dirty secret is that everyone,
especially the famous,
are just making it up as they go along.

There is no perfection, only progress.
Done is much better than perfect.

⌁ · ❖ · ⌁

You choose to be lucky by believing that
any setbacks are just temporary.

If nobody else does
what you do,
you won't need a resume.

To lower tensions during a dispute,
mirror the other person's body language.

———

For a great payoff,
be especially curious
about the things you are not interested in.

———

It is not hard to identify a thief:
It is the one who believes
that everybody steals.

We are unconsciously distracted by seeing our reflection. You can alleviate a lot of the fatigue of teleconferencing all day if you turn off your self-view.

Read the books
that your favorite authors once read.

When you can't decide,
ask yourself, "Which choice
will pay off more later than now?"
The easy choice pays off right away.
The best choice will pay off at the end.

As long as an idea stays in your head
it is perfect.
But perfect things are never real.
Immediately put an idea down into words,
or in a sketch, or as a cardboard prototype.
Now your idea is much closer to reality
because it is imperfect.

Trust the 3-star product reviews because they
tell both the good and the bad, which is the
real state for most things.

First, always ask for what you want.
Works in relationships, business, life.

Even if you don't say anything,
if you listen carefully,
people will consider you
a great conversationalist.

Curiosity is fatal to certainty.
The more curious you are,
the less certain you'll be.

Measure your wealth
not by the things you can buy
but by the things that no money can buy.

⌒⌒⌒ · ◈ · ⌒⌒⌒

To learn from your mistakes,
first laugh at your mistakes.

⌒⌒⌒ · ◈ · ⌒⌒⌒

It's unfortunate when someone you
carefully trained leaves; but it is worse if
you don't train them and they stay.

Your opinion on a contentious issue
gains power when you can argue
the opposite side as well as they can.

When you keep people waiting,
they begin to think of all your flaws.

Trust is earned in drops
and lost in buckets.
Unwavering honesty will help seal in trust.

An honest friend is someone
who wants nothing at all from you.

⸺ ·❖· ⸺

You will spend one third of your life
in your bed sleeping,
and almost another third
in your chair sitting.
It's worth investing in a great bed
and fantastic chair.

⸺ ·❖· ⸺

The purpose of listening
is not to reply,
but to hear what is not being said.

Don't spoil a movie
you are sure to see
by watching the trailer.
Only watch trailers for movies
you are unsure of,
or unlikely to see.

⌐———·◦·———⌐

Your best teacher is your last mistake.

⌐———·◦·———⌐

On the dashboard of every gasoline car
is a symbol of gas pump with a little arrow.
The arrow points to the side of the car
that accesses your gas tank.
Remember this when you borrow or rent a car.

The perfect kind of art
to display in your home
are odd pieces
that a child is unlikely to forget.

Spending as little as 15 minutes
(1% of your day)
on improving how you do your thing,
is the most powerful way
to amplify and advance your thing.

Instead of asking your child
what they learned today,
ask them who they helped today.

The greatest killer of happiness
is comparison.
If you must compare,
compare yourself to you yesterday.

Your 20s are the perfect time
to do a few things that are
unusual, weird, bold, risky, unexplainable,
crazy, unprofitable,
and look nothing like "success."
For the rest of your life
these experiences will serve
as your muse.

Don't define yourself
by your opinions,
because then you can't change your mind.
Define yourself by your values.

⌐————— · ◈ · —————⌐

To succeed once,
focus on the outcome;
to keep succeeding,
focus on the process
that makes the outcome.

Your ideal partner
is not someone you never disagree with
but someone you are glad to disagree with.

An open heart is the most
direct path to an open mind.

If you are stuck in life,
travel to a place you have never heard of.

Being curious
about another person's view is the most
powerful way to change their view.

If you don't care about your people,
they won't care about your mission.

To speed a meeting up,
require that any person who speaks
must say something
no one else in the room knows.

The rich have money.

The wealthy have time.

It is easier to become wealthy than rich.

If you want to go fast, go alone;
if you want to go further, go together.

Your best photo portrait will be taken
not while you are smiling
but when you are quiet
a moment after you have been laughing.
Use a photographer who makes you laugh.

If your sense of responsibility
is not expanding as you grow,
you are not really growing.

When making plans,
you must allow yourself
to get lost
in order to find the thing
you didn't know you were looking for.

The natural state of all possessions
is to need repair and maintenance.
What you own will eventually own you.
Choose selectively.

⌐——— ◦ ——⌐

To write about something hard to explain,
write a detailed letter to a friend about why it is so
hard to explain, and
then remove the initial "Dear Friend" part
and you'll have a great first draft.

Commit to doing no work,

no business,

no income one day a week.

Call it a sabbath (or not).

Use that day

for resting, recharging, and cultivating

the most important things in life.

Counterintuitively, this sabbath will prove

to be your most productive act all week.

⌒⌒⌒ · ❦ · ⌒⌒⌒

Embrace pronoia,

which is the opposite of paranoia.

Choose to believe that

the entire universe is conspiring

behind your back

to make you a success.

Go with the option that
opens up yet more options.

⟨⸺ ⁕ ⊛ ⁕ ⸺⟩

The first step
is usually to complete the last step.
You can't load into a full dish rack.

⟨⸺ ⁕ ⊛ ⁕ ⸺⟩

When you are stuck, make a long list of
everything that *cannot* possibly work.
On that list will be a seed that
leads to a solution that will work.

Right now,

no matter your age,

these are your golden years.

The good stuff will yield golden memories

and the bad stuff will yield golden lessons.

The most effective remedy for anger is delay.

Re-visioning the ordinary

is what art, literature, and comedy do.

You can elevate mundane details

into magical wonders

simply by noticing them.

Aim to die broke.

Give to your beneficiaries before you die;

it's more fun and useful to them.

Spend it all.

Your last check should go to the funeral

home and it should bounce.

See that old person taking forever in line?

That is the future you. Have patience.

Invent as many family rituals
as you can handle with ease.
Anything done on a schedule
—large or small, significant or silly—
can become a ritual.
Repeated consistently,
small routines become legendary.
Anticipation is key.

The chief prevention against getting old
is to remain astonished.

Art before laundry.

⸻ ⬥ ⸻

Life lessons will be presented to you
in the order they are needed.
Everything you need to master the lesson
is within you.
Once you have truly learned a lesson,
you will be presented with the next one.
If you are alive,
that means you still have lessons to learn.

———— ·❖· ————

Very few regrets in life are about
what you did. Almost all are about
what you didn't do.

Your goal is to be able to say,

on the day before you die

that you have fully become yourself.

⌐⌐⌐⌐ ⌐ ⊚ ⌐ ⌐⌐⌐⌐

Advice like these are not laws.

They are like hats.

If one doesn't fit, try another.

ACKNOWLEDGMENTS

Paul Slovak   editor
Amanda Dewey   designer
Jason Ramirez   cover artist
John Brockman   literary agent
Claudia Dawson   producer
Camille Hartsell   fact-checker
Shelby Meizlik   publicist
Lydia Hirt   marketer
Hugh Howey   early reader

The author can be reached at kk@kk.org,
or at his website kk.org.